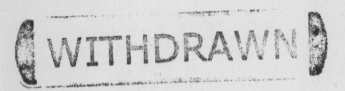

One Hundred Years
OF PUBLISHING

Thirty-four Beacon Street

One Hundred Years

OF PUBLISHING

1837 ∾ 1937

THIRTY-FOUR BEACON STREET

LITTLE, BROWN AND COMPANY

BOSTON

And books, we know, are a
Substantial World (both pure and good)
—WORDSWORTH

Illustrations

One Hundred Years
OF PUBLISHING

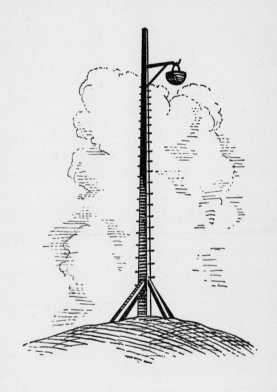

OLD BEACON OF 1635
ON SENTINEL (BEACON) HILL

I

IN 1837 Boston was still a provincial city, but was soon to become "The Hub of the Universe" according to Oliver Wendell Holmes, who came into the practice of medicine just at the time that Charles C. Little and James Brown entered into partnership for the purposes of publishing and selling books.

In that same year one could catch a glimpse of young Doctor Holmes driving about the city in that chaise which, he asserted gayly, brought him more satisfaction than did the active practice of medicine which he had just begun. Ralph Waldo Emerson, who was born a Bostonian, had resigned his pastorate of the Second Church of Boston five years before and was living in Concord and appearing before the public as a lecturer; his first home was not very far from Little and Brown's on Washington Street. James Russell Lowell was still a student at Harvard, but he had already shown his talents for writing as one of the editors of *Harvardiana*.

William Lloyd Garrison's *Liberator* was six years old, William Ellery Channing had published his carefully considered book against slavery and Wendell Phillips was testing his oratory; while Whittier came and went both as agent of the New England Anti-Slavery Society and as editor.

These men of letters, however, were still in the making. Longfellow was buried in his books, Hawthorne was trying to live by his pen and finding it impossible, Thoreau was just beginning his series of diaries, William Hickling Prescott had just finished "Ferdinand and Isabella," on which he had worked ten years, Richard Henry Dana graduated that year from Harvard College; while Charles Sprague, who had welcomed Lafayette to Boston in verse, had won his reputation as the Banker Poet of Boston.

Boston at this time, with a population of 80,000, had not grown far beyond the limits of the old town in British days, but the years from 1821 on had developed great changes in the appearance of the city. The State House graced the abbreviated top of Beacon Hill, with The Athenæum close at hand. The mansion house of John Hancock adjoining the State House was one of the sights of the city until it was torn down in 1863, heroic efforts of citizens to secure its preservation by the State as a permanent memorial having failed. Next door, at 31 Beacon Street, Samuel A. Eliot, Mayor of Boston, lived in 1837; there his son Charles William Eliot, was born three years earlier. Three doors farther down the Hill, at the corner of Joy Street, was the house of Nathaniel Pope Russell, now the home of Little, Brown and Company. Beacon Street itself stretched outward toward the Mill Dam and the filling in of the Back Bay District was soon to be agitated.

The business section was still clustered about State Street, stretching down to the wharves and over beyond Faneuil Hall

advertising and tiny circulation. There were at different times between 1830 and 1840 fifteen daily papers, and at one time twelve of these were being issued. Of the fifteen, four are now in existence: the *Transcript*, the *Post*, the *Traveler* and the *Advertiser*. In special fields *Zion's Herald* was popular, while the *Christian Register* was slowly making its way. And by far the most remarkable of the Boston papers — Garrison's anti-slavery *Liberator* — had already begun to have its effect not only upon Boston but upon the country.

The ascendancy of Massachusetts, and of Boston particularly, to literary supremacy was due in part to the two great movements which stirred New England at about this time — transcendentalism, with Emerson, Thoreau and Bronson Alcott as its leaders, and abolitionism, with William Lloyd Garrison, Whittier and Wendell Phillips its champions. Already the Symposium, an informal association, had been organized; the Brook Farm community was soon to be formed, and the *Dial* to appear as the organ of its new philosophy.

Yes, Boston was entering an era of intense mental activity. To those who have already been mentioned was soon to be added Samuel Gridley Howe, who married Julia Ward and whose fame became overshadowed by his wife's. There were Charles Sumner, the statesman, Thomas Appleton, famous for his quips, Elizabeth Peabody and Horace Mann, eager for educational advancement. Those were the days of soirées when these little groups met and discussed cultural development. There were Lyceums which were thronged with eager and expectant audiences. The Saturday Club soon came to hold the lead in intellectual development. Motley and Parkman were to establish their reputations as historians; Charles Eliot Norton, Thomas Wentworth Higginson and Edward Everett Hale were to provide their own special niches. The realm of letters was to be dominated by these little groups, most of them having originated at Harvard College across the river.

II

THE years following 1820 constituted a period of preparation for the great literature which was to come from the New England authors after the Civil War, and it was to the established booksellers and publishers of that day that the harvest of new publications came in the succeeding years.

Naturally the bookstores became general meeting places and into this stimulating environment came Messrs. Little and Brown, in 1837, while diagonally across Washington Street at the Old Corner Book Store William D. Ticknor had put up his sign and had as clerk one James T. Fields.

Little, Brown and Company have for one hundred years operated under the names of

CHARLES C.
LITTLE

JAMES BROWN

the founders, Charles C. Little and James
Brown. Their early inheritance in the book
field dates back to 1784 when Ebenezer
Battelle opened a little bookstore on Marl-
borough Street, Boston, now that part of
Washington Street which is between School
and Eliot. This business was conducted by
various individuals, until in 1813 it passed
into the hands of Jacob A. Cummings, who
taught a private school in Cambridge, and
William Hilliard, proprietor of the Harvard
University Book Store. In 1821 the firm
name became
Carter, Hilliard &
Company, and
Timothy Carter,
who had come in
as an apprentice,
ran the store. He
engaged Charles C.
Little as a clerk.
When Mr. Carter
withdrew from the
firm, Harrison Gray
came in and in 1827
a new firm, under

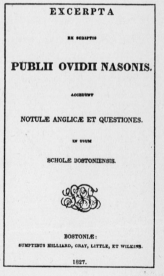

EXCERPTA

EX SCRIPTIS

PUBLII OVIDII NASONIS.

ACCEDUNT

NOTULÆ ANGLICÆ ET QUESTIONES.

IN USUM

SCHOLÆ BOSTONIENSIS.

BOSTONIÆ:
SUMPTIBUS HILLIARD, GRAY, LITTLE, ET WILKINS.

1827.

the title of Hilliard, Gray & Company, was formed. Charles C. Little was a partner during some part of the next ten years and for a time the firm name was Hilliard, Gray, Little, and Wilkins. Meanwhile James Brown, who had begun work in Mr. Hilliard's Cambridge bookstore in 1818, had become his partner in 1826, then had acquired an interest in the firm of Hilliard, Gray & Company in Boston. Apparently the two companies were closely affiliated for a time, and one must suppose that during this period Mr. Little, who married Hilliard's daughter in 1829, and Mr. Brown had become very close friends.

The *Daily Advertiser* of June 29, 1837, contains three small advertisements:

NOTICE.—The copartnership heretofore existing between the subscribers, under the firm of HILLIARD, GRAY & CO. is hereby dissolved by mutual consent. H. GRAY and CHARLES BROWN are authorized to adjust the concerns of said firm.

HARRISON GRAY,
JAMES BROWN,
CHARLES BROWN.

Boston, June 22, 1837.   Je 29

COPARTNERSHIP. — The undersigned will continue the Publishing and Bookselling business, under the firm of HILLIARD, GRAY & CO. at the new building, Water street, corner of Devonshire.

HARRISON GRAY,
CHARLES BROWN.

Boston, June 22, 1837.   Je 29

COPARTNERSHIP NOTICE. — The undersigned have formed a copartnership, under the firm of CHARLES C. LITTLE & CO., for the purpose of Publishing, Importing and Selling Books, and have taken the old stand of Hilliard, Gray & Co., No. 112, Washington street, and purchased their Law, Foreign and Miscellaneous stock.

CHARLES C. LITTLE,
JAMES BROWN.

Je 29   istf

The new firm acquired the bookstore at 112 (now 254) Washington Street and the stock and rights of all the general and legal

LITTLE, BROWN AND COMPANY'S
FIRST HOME AT 112 WASHINGTON STREET

titles, while subsequent advertisements of Harrison Gray and Charles Brown indicate that their new company dealt chiefly in schoolbooks.

Among the assets of the Hilliard, Gray &

Company business secured by Messrs. Little
and Brown at this time were certain uncom-
pleted publishing projects: the series of Amer-

A RETAIL SALE TO WENDELL PHILLIPS

ican biographies, the Works of Benjamin
Franklin and the Writings of George Washington, all edited by Jared Sparks; George
Bancroft's "History of the United States";
and a number of other important enterprises.
An examination of the earliest catalogues of
the company reveals the fact that the first
volume to be written by James Russell
Lowell, "A Year's Life," was published under
the Little and Brown imprint in 1841. Other

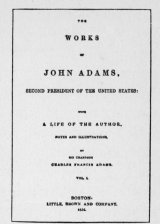

important works undertaken by the concern in its earlier years were "Manual of Political Ethics" by Francis Lieber, "The Letters of John Adams" and those of his wife Abigail, both edited by his grandson Charles Francis Adams, and the writings and speeches of Daniel Webster, edited by Edward Everett.

This is ample evidence that the firm from its beginning devoted its attention to publishing as well as bookselling. Its name always appeared in the imprint on title-pages as Charles C. Little and James Brown until 1847, when it became Little, Brown and Company.

The early issues of the Boston papers contain many announcements of the importations of rare and beautiful editions of English classics, of translations of the noted works published in France, in Spain and in Germany. Looking through one of the early catalogues issued by the house, one finds a rich store of fascinating reading in English literature. Yet we find numerous items in Latin, showing that a gentleman's library must needs still contain a sprinkling of the classics in the original. The announcements of the new and forthcoming American publications were always placed at the end of these pamphlets as if American publishers were timid of exhibiting their own wares. Special prominence was given to the legal publications, and quite properly, for the company was for many years the leading publisher of law books in the entire country.

It may not be amiss at this point to include a brief word about the two gentlemen whose names have carried through a century of publishing, a record unequalled in New England and only surpassed by the Harper and Apple-

ton imprints in New York and that of Lippin-
cott in Philadelphia.

Charles C. Little was born on July 25,
1799, in Kennebunk, Maine. He left his na-
tive state as a youth to secure employment in
Boston, and spent a short time in a shipping-
house before entering the book business. He
gave much of his time to the legal publications of the firm, and it was chiefly through
his efforts that Little and Brown became the
foremost house in America in this field. They
took over from Hilliard, Gray & Company
the first three or four of Judge Joseph Story's
works and soon issued others; then came the
first great American work on Evidence, by
Simon Greenleaf. When Professor Greenleaf's
treatise was being published, ninety years or
so ago, the *London Law Magazine* paid a nota-
ble tribute to him and to Story, saying: "It is
no mean honor to America that her schools of
jurisprudence have produced two of the first
writers and finest authorities of this century
— the great and good man who has just been
taken from us (Judge Joseph Story) and his
worthy and eminent associate, Professor

SIMON GREENLEAF

JOSEPH STORY

Greenleaf. Upon the existing law of contracts and the law of evidence more light has shone from the new world than from all the lawyers who adorn the courts of Europe."

Mr. Little was active as a capitalist and, to some extent, in public affairs. He was a large owner of real estate in Cambridge. He was instrumental in introducing three great improvements in that city, water from Fresh Pond, the horse railroad and the gas light; and at the time of his death in 1869 he was president of the Charles River National Bank.

The resolutions passed at his death, which are to be found in the papers of the day, indicate that he was highly respected in all walks of business, both in Boston and in Cambridge.

James Brown was born in Acton, Massachusetts, on May 19, 1800, of sturdy New England stock. His father died when the boy was only thirteen, and the widow's means were insufficient to keep the household together, so the boys of the family had to find work, and James went to live with a neighboring farmer. In 1815 he came to Cambridge in search of employment and found a situation as domestic in the family of a professor, where while he performed his household duties he was instructed in mathematics and Latin by his employer. When he was eighteen, as a result of Professor Hedge's recommendation, he was offered and accepted a position as salesman and general assistant to Mr. William Hilliard in the University Book Store and thus found an occupation which suited his tastes. From that date on, his chief interest in life was literature, and he satisfied Mr. Hilliard so well that in 1826 he was offered a partnership. After he and Mr. Little began their copartnership, the general publishing and the importation of foreign books at Little and Brown's came under Mr. Brown's control. For this he was well fitted. He knew the worth and the value of books, and had an intuitive sagacity in discerning what the public of that time wanted. In this connection a quotation from "A Memoir of James Brown," by George Stillman Hillard, privately printed in 1856, deserves mention:

"Their (Little and Brown's) publications in general literature have been, for the most part, of a grave, solid, and substantial character, such as works in theology, history, politics, political economy, and biography — rarely meddling with those lighter and more ephemeral publications that come with the leaves of spring and go with the leaves of autumn." The house published no novels in those days.

During the last fourteen years of his life Mr. Brown made five voyages to Europe. John Murray, the English publisher, became his close friend, and for him Mr. Brown's youngest son was named. At home, his interests were many and varied, and his personality and charm made him welcome among the literary and artistic circles of both Cambridge and Boston, where he was a Trustee of the Massachusetts Agricultural Society, a Trustee of the Boston Athenæum and a member of various other societies. His own personal library was extensive and well selected. The Athenæum was a beneficiary from this collection. Following his death, in 1855, resolutions were passed by many associations, including the booksellers of Boston and the publishing trade in New York.

LAWS OF THE UNITED STATES.

MESSAGE

FROM

THE PRESIDENT OF THE UNITED STATES,

TRANSMITTING

A communication of the Attorney General relative to a contract with Messrs. Little & Brown for certain copies of the Laws and Treaties of the United States, in pursuance of a joint resolution of the House of Representatives of March 3, 1845.

FEBRUARY 17, 1846.
Read, and referred to the Committee of Ways and Means.

To the Senate and House of Representatives:

I herewith transmit a communication from the Attorney General, relating to a contract entered into by him with Messrs. Little & Brown for certain copies of their proposed edition of the Laws and Treaties of the United States, in pursuance of the joint resolution of 3d March, 1845.

JAMES K. POLK.

WASHINGTON, *February* 16, 1846.

ATTORNEY GENERAL'S OFFICE,
February 10, 1846.

SIR: I have the honor to communicate to you, for the information of the Senate and House of Representatives of the United States, that, in pursuance of authority vested in the Attorney General by the joint resolution of 3d March, 1845, I entered into a contract with Messrs. Little & Brown, of Boston, for one thousand copies of their proposed edition of the Laws and Treaties of the United States, and for such additional copies of the work as the government may from time to time require to be furnished.

I enclose two copies of the agreement, with the stipulation for its faithful performance. The originals have been filed with the First Comptroller of the Treasury.

In the execution of their work, the publishers have freely communicated with me, and have exhibited satisfactory proofs to me of their having taken

Ritchie & Heiss, print.

A PAGE FROM CONGRESSIONAL
RECORD OF 1846

III

DURING its first ten years the company remained unchanged, developing the publication of standard and serious books, increasing the activities of its law book department and maintaining its reputation in bookselling and importing. Then, in 1847, the name was changed from Charles C. Little and James Brown to Little, Brown and Company, with Augustus Flagg as junior partner. From 1869, when Mr. Little died, to the time of his retirement from business Mr. Flagg was the managing partner. He was a man of rare ability and fine judgment, and saw the company through the depression of the seventies with each depression year showing some profit. Little, Brown and Company were publishers of Prescott's "Ferdinand and Isabella" for several years, beginning in 1838. They ceased to publish it when a New York publisher offered higher royalties. Subsequently Phillips, Sampson & Company, of Boston, offered still higher royalties and became Prescott's publishers. Referring to this Mr. Flagg said some years later:

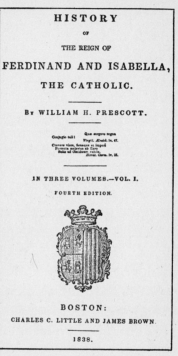

"Mr. Sampson came to see me one day, and we talked about book publishing. I told him, among other things, there is a great difference in publishers; some are inclined to pay, what I call, 'Money for glory.' 'Yes,' said Sampson, 'I know that; I have paid twenty thousand dollars, more or less, for glory. There is no money in it.' 'That

won't do,' said I. 'When Prescott's folks came
in and wanted me to take his histories, I told
them I would advance a thousand dollars a
volume copyright, but I could not afford to

AUGUSTUS FLAGG

pay any glory money, as I thought I had
made sufficient reputation, and I preferred
to have less glory than to have my notes go
to protest.' The troubles of 1857 had taught
me a lesson. At that time most every promi-
nent house was obliged to take up both sides
of the bill-book. I made up my mind if I ever
got through that year, I would so shape the
concern as to get along without giving notes,
and from that time we have never asked a

cent of discount or borrowed any money. The best investment a man can make is to pay his debts, and after that he can make any investment he likes."

One of the firm's most ambitious undertakings, begun in 1853, was its series of British Poets, from Spenser to Moore. These were not importations; the volumes were printed in Cambridge by John Wilson and Son, H. O. Houghton and other printers. By 1858 the series comprised ninety-six volumes, with thirty-one more in press, and by this time the sub-title had become "From Chaucer to Wordsworth." Quoting from the catalogue: "The size and style of the volumes are those of PICKERING'S ALDINE POETS" (published in England) "and such of the works of that edition as fall entirely within the plan of the present collection will be embodied in it. Each separate work is sold by itself and the price of each volume, bound in the Aldine style, or in cloth, gilt lettered, is 75 cents." The series was edited by Francis J. Child, Boylston Professor of Rhetoric and Oratory in Harvard College.

In 1855 John Bartlett, of Cambridge, pub-

MISCELLANEOUS WORKS.

Terms, six months credit; discount 25 per cent. except on prices marked *net*.

ADAMS'S (John) Life and Works. Complete. Edited by
    C. F. Adams. 10 vols. 8vo. Cloth $22.50
    ——————— 10 vols. Royal 8vo. . . 30.00

AGASSIZ' Contributions to the Natural History of the
    United States of America. To be completed in 10 vols. 4to.
    Plates. Cloth . . . . *net* 120.00

    Vol. I. containing — I. An Essay on Classification. II. A Revision
    of the North American Turtle. III. The Embryology of these
    Animals, with plates. Now ready . . . . . *net* 12.00

No subscriptions taken excepting for the work complete.

AMERICAN ALMANAC, 1849, '50, '51, '52, '53. 12mo.
    Stitched, per vol. 1.00

AMERICAN LOYALISTS, (The) or Biographical Sketches
    of Adherents of the British Crown in the War of the Revolution.
    By Lorenzo Sabine. 8vo. Cloth 2.50

AMES'S (Fisher) Life and Works. New edition, revised.
    2 vols. 8vo. Cloth 4.50
    ——————————— Half calf, . . . *net* 5.20
    ——————————— Full calf, . . . *net* 6.00

BACON'S Essays, and Wisdom of the Ancients. 16mo. . .75
    ——————————— Half calf, extra gilt 1.50
    ——————————— Full calf, " " 1.75

BANCROFT'S History of the United States. 3 vols. 8vo.
    Cloth 6.00

    ——————————— Vols. IV., V., and VI.
    (Comprising the History of the Causes of the Revolution.) 8vo.
    Cloth, per vol. . . . . *net* 1.69

    ——————————— 6 vols. 8vo. Sheep.
    Library style 14.25

☞ *If 75 volumes, (in cloth or sheep binding,) are taken at one time, a discount of
one third will be allowed.*

    ——————————— 6 vols. 8vo. Half
    calf, gilt, marbled edges . . . . . *net* 15.00
    ——————————— Half calf, antique . . *net* 15.00
    ——————————— Full calf, gilt, marbled edges *net* 17.40
    ——————————— Full calf, antique . . *net* 17.40

A PAGE FROM THE CATALOGUE OF 1857

lished the first edition of his "Familiar Quotations." He, like James Brown, secured his early training in the University Book Store in Cambridge, which he owned and managed from 1849 until 1859. Then he became a partner in Little, Brown and Company and the firm took over the publication of his remarkable book. He revised it eight times, through the publication of the ninth edition in 1891. It is fitting that the company is issuing a new edition, the eleventh, in its centenary year, and the happy choice of Christopher Morley as editor and Louella Everett, who is widely known through her "Notes and Queries" contributions in the *New York Times* and the *Boston Transcript*, as associate editor, is a pledge of its permanent value.

It is interesting to note that as early as 1857 the little group of publishers and writers were a closely knit unit, intimate in their social as well as their business lives. John Townsend Trowbridge in his article, "An Early Contributor's Recollections," wrote: "In the latter part of October, 1857, when the first number of the *Atlantic* had been out a day or two, I went one evening to take a hand at whist with Francis Henry Underwood, John Bartlett, and a young man I will call The Fourth Hand, who remarked as we took our

JOHN BARTLETT

places around the table, 'Gentlemen, what say you? Let's not play whist! I'd rather spend the evening talking about the *Atlantic Monthly*.' "

The magazine had just made its first appearance with the November issue, 1857. Published by Phillips, Sampson and Company, it was sponsored very largely by Underwood, the firm's "literary adviser", and was edited by James Russell Lowell, who at this time wrote to Charles Eliot Norton, then in England: "The magazine is to be free without being fanatical, and we hope to unite in it all available talent of all modes of opinion. The magazine is to have opinions of its own and not be afraid to speak them."

And so was launched the magazine which has held its high reputation under a succession of distinguished editors. Soon the *Atlantic* became famous for its dinners as well as its pages. The writers and editors of the country for years enjoyed its hospitality and opportunities unique for the exchange of thought and opinion.

Arthur Gilman in his *Atlantic* article on "Atlantic Dinners and Diners" writes about the first dinner: "Who were present on this occasion, for which we should be so grateful? A dozen literary gentlemen had been asked to come, and at the head of the table sat Mr. Phillips, of the publishing firm. At the foot was Mr. Underwood, 'literary adviser', who had pressed the matter to a fruitful issue. Mr. Longfellow, then fifty years of age, Dr. Holmes, two years younger, the historian Motley, five years younger, Mr. Lowell, only thirty-eight, Ralph Waldo Emerson, and John Eliot Cabot were there. Mr. Underwood told me that Harriet Beecher Stowe was the person whose urgency had effectually influenced Mr. Phillips, but neither she nor any other lady was present at this initial dinner."

Sixty-eight years later Little, Brown and Company acquired the book publishing business of the *Atlantic Monthly*, which had been begun in 1917, a few years after Ellery Sedgwick bought the magazine, with an arrangement for a permanent association which was to give many important books the Little, Brown imprint.

John Murray Brown, the youngest son of James Brown, became the active head of the firm after Mr. Flagg's retirement in 1884, and in the late nineties his partners were Charles W. Allen, James W. McIntyre and Hulings C. Brown. During the regime of Mr. Flagg, the firm seems to have been interested primarily in its law list and its importations, and issued very little in the way of biography and history, though it began the publication of Francis Parkman's books in 1865. In this connection it is interesting to note that its bulletin of November, 1878, contains the following: "ENCYCLOPÆDIA BRITANNICA. — Little, Brown & Co. are the American agents for the original and authoritative issue of the ninth edition of this standard work, now in course of publication. This edition is the first and clearest impression, on paper of wide margins, and is delivered here in advance of reprints. Eight volumes, out of the twenty-one which will constitute the edition, are now published, and the others will follow at intervals of about four months." And its catalogues of the 1850's list the Eighth Edition with the line "Messrs. L. B. & Co. are the sole agents for the sale of this work in this country."

Now, in the nineties, it had begun to expand in the general publishing field. It had issued choice editions of Bulwer and Marryat

FRANCIS PARKMAN

JOHN MURRAY BROWN

ADMIRAL A. T. MAHAN

JEREMIAH CURTIN AND HENRYK SIENKIEWICZ

and translations of Alexandre Dumas, Alphonse Daudet and Victor Hugo, and was publishing the writings of Admiral A. T. Mahan. It had entered the fiction field at last, and in 1896 published "Quo Vadis," by Henryk Sienkiewicz, the best seller of the period. Jeremiah Curtin introduced the work of Sienkiewicz to its future publisher. Mr. Curtin has been called the greatest linguist this country has ever produced. He convinced Mr. John Murray Brown and Mr. McIntyre of Sienkiewicz's importance and in 1890 his translation of Sienkiewicz's "With Fire and Sword" was published. Sienkiewicz was unknown in the United States and the sale of "With Fire and Sword" in its first year was only 1922 copies. The Polish names, Hmelnitski, Skshetuski, Vishnyevetski, Zaiontchkovski, bothered American readers. Next came "The Deluge," in 1891, which sold only 1585 copies in two years. The third novel in the trilogy, "Pan Michael," was issued in 1893 and sold 1655 copies that year and 777 the next. This must have been most discouraging; patience was needed and fortunately Mr. Brown and Mr. McIntyre kept

"DRYGOODS ECONOMIST"
ADVERTISEMENT
MAY, 1898

their belief in the greatness of Sienkiewicz. At last, in 1896, "Quo Vadis, a Narrative of the Time of Nero," appeared and swept the country in editions ranging from the two-volume de luxe edition of two hundred and fifty sets retailing at $12.00, to the paper-bound edition which was wholesaled as low as nine cents per copy in the fight between Little, Brown and Company and the publishers of another translation. Under the then existing copyright law, the original Polish work could not be protected in the United States unless a text in Polish were published here within six months of publication in Poland. Naturally this was not done, with the result that in December, 1897, another translation was issued by Altemus, of Philadelphia, and the battle began. The author, of course, received no royalties from the other translation. "Quo Vadis" made Sienkiewicz famous in the United States with the result that his historical romances of Poland, which many critics would put above the more popular book, immediately began to secure the wide reading which they deserved.

COPYRIGHT PAGE OF THE NEW EDITION
OF "THE BOSTON COOKING-SCHOOL
COOK BOOK"

Eighteen hundred and ninety-six also marked the first appearance of "The Boston Cooking-School Cook Book," by Fannie Merritt Farmer, which took its place as the leading American cook book, which it still holds, with total sales in excess of 1,700,000 copies.

Two years later the firm purchased the general list of Roberts Brothers and thus acquired a distinguished and successful group of authors — a number of them dating back to the early days when Boston held the center of the literary stage. Edward Everett Hale with his "The Man Without a Country," Balzac in Miss Wormeley's wonderful translations, Helen Hunt Jackson, author of "Ramona," Laura E. Richards, Susan Coolidge, Emily Dickinson, Mary P. Wells Smith and a host of other authors came under the Little, Brown imprint; but most important of all was Louisa May Alcott with her many charming and delightful books for children, chief among them "Little Women," which has maintained its popularity up to the present day and still retains the title of America's Most

EDWARD EVERETT HALE

HELEN HUNT JACKSON

Popular Juvenile. Her books alone, as it turned out, were worth the price paid for the business.

The enterprising manager of the Boston firm of Roberts Brothers was Thomas Niles, who began his career as a clerk in the Old Corner Book Store in 1839. Entering the employ of the new firm in the 1860's, he shortly became a partner of the Roberts brothers, and it was Mr. Niles who was largely responsible for Miss Alcott's successful career. After she had had indifferent success with her earlier work, Mr. Niles asked Miss Alcott to write a girl's book and an old idea of "The Pathetic Family," based on the Alcotts, recurred to her mind. She set herself to describe her early home life. She finished the story during the summer of 1868 after Mr. Niles had expressed disappointment when he read the first twelve chapters. Now he read the entire manuscript and was doubtful; but wisely he showed it to his niece, then to other girls, and they all loved it. So the first part of "Little Women" was published that autumn. Mr. Niles made Miss Alcott an outright offer for the publishing rights, but at the same time advised her not to part with them. She ac-

LOUISA MAY ALCOTT
From a daguerreotype taken about 1862

cepted a royalty on all copies sold, and in her journal, in 1885, she wrote this comment:

"An honest publisher and a lucky author, for the copyright made her fortune and the

(*43*)

'dull book' was the first golden egg of the ugly duckling.''

The book was a great success and was followed by the sequel, or second part, then by other stories.

Four years after Mr. Niles' death, the business of Roberts Brothers was acquired by Little, Brown and Company. Now, twelve years after the expiration of the copyright, the company is paying royalties to Miss Alcott's heirs on its own editions of "Little Women" and on those issued by other publishers with its approval.

Almost from its beginning the house was a leader in law book publishing, and this department of the business was at its peak in the last quarter of the nineteenth century.

In 1878 Little, Brown and Company began the publication of a law book bulletin. In the first issue may be found a list of its law books then in print, and in addition to the works of Story and Greenleaf, who have already been mentioned, one finds volumes by Melville M. Bigelow, Thomas M. Cooley, Edmund I.

Daniell, Theophilus Parsons, Jarus W. Perry and Emory Washburn. The firm was then the official publisher of the *American Law Review*, the Massachusetts Statutes and Supreme Court Reports and the United States Supreme Court Digest and Statutes at Large. In the same issue of the bulletin is an announcement of a new "Law Students' Series" which contains the statement: "Strange to say, in a country where there are probably two thousand young men entering every year the study of the law, there has been up to this time no systematic and thorough series of elementary treatises of the size and style especially convenient for students." The close contacts of Little, Brown and Company and the teaching staff of the Harvard Law School at the time are indicated by the list of books in this series announced in the bulletin, for of the six authors named, three were C. C. Langdell, Dane Professor of Law at the Harvard Law School, J. B. Thayer, Royall Professor of Law and J. B. Ames, Professor of Law.

In later years we find listed in the bulletin other volumes which to-day serve their useful purposes: for example, "The Common Law" by Oliver Wendell Holmes, Jr., John F. Dillon's great treatise on Municipal Corporations, and John T. Morse, Jr.'s "The Laws of

OLIVER WENDELL HOLMES, JR.

Banks and Banking." It is interesting also to see listed a treatise upon the Transfer of Stock, by A. Lawrence Lowell and Francis C. Lowell (published in 1885), and one on Telegraph Communication, by Morris Gray, published at about the same time. Particular mention should be made also of Joseph H. Beale's treatise on Criminal Pleading, John Chipman Gray's "The Rule Against Per-

JOHN F. DILLON

petuities" and Samuel Williston's "Cases on Contracts."

While the connection with the Harvard Law School was close, Little, Brown's affiliations were scattered throughout the country.

The bulletin contains news of the various law schools in the West as well as in the East and the roster of authors includes names of distinction far and wide.

On to-day's list will be found many of these same volumes, revised to date, indicating the permanence and the authority which they possess. Perhaps the most distinguished as well as the most popular legal writer on the Little, Brown law list to-day is John H. Wigmore, whose Treatise on Evidence, Code of Evidence, Cases on Evidence, Cases on Torts and Principles of Judicial Proof are leading authorities. Another writer of high reputation to be mentioned is Charles Cheney Hyde, whose great work on International Law is the American authority. The company also publishes several series, including those on Continental Legal History, Criminal Science, The Evolution of Law, and the "Essays in Anglo-American Legal History."

JOHN H. WIGMORE

IV

THUS with the turn of the century Little, Brown and Company was securely entrenched in its position as one of the leading publishers of the country in the general field, and it had as well one of the most substantial law lists in America and a large retail book store. A subscription department had been added to supplement the bookstore sales of its own sets, and the company was still operating from the original location at 254 Washington Street, but in a larger and more commodious building, the property of Harvard College.

Changes, however, were soon to follow.
James W. McIntyre, who had begun working
for the company in 1865, at the age of six-

JAMES W. McINTYRE

teen, had eventually shown unusual abilities
as a publisher, much to the gratification of
Mr. Brown, who turned many of his responsi-
bilities over to the younger man. After he

had persuaded his associates that the Roberts Brothers business should be acquired, Mr. McIntyre assumed complete charge of the publishing department, and following Mr. Brown's death in 1908 he became the active head of the firm.

The thoughts and the tastes of American readers were changing and the firm recognized this change and kept pace with it. Boston also had changed. The Washington Street store was now far from the shopping district. It was convenient to bankers and lawyers who had their offices adjacent, to be sure; but the rank and file of shoppers, especially the women, no longer patronized lower Washington Street. Furthermore, the firm had so increased its general publishing business and its national circulation of books that its interest in the bookstore had inevitably lessened. Indeed, publishing had become more and more a specialist's work, so that the two fields, publishing and bookselling, had grown apart. Recognizing this condition and realizing the need for larger quarters for the publishing departments, the company purchased the Cabot family residence at 34 Beacon Street, on the corner of Joy Street, where it established itself in 1909.

After the death of James W. McIntyre in 1913 the business was incorporated, with the eldest partner, Charles W. Allen (whose connection with the house dated back to 1869)

CHARLES W. ALLEN

as president. He was succeeded by Alfred R. McIntyre, son of the elder McIntyre, who has guided the destinies of the company through periods of national prosperity and widespread depression. Mr. McIntyre was born in 1886, began work for the house after his graduation from Harvard College in 1907, and served as its vice president and general

COLOPHONS
USED SINCE
1837

manager for several years before becoming its president in 1926. He is a sincere believer in the publishing policy which is expressed by the phrase "Fewer and better books," or as it appears in the colophon which at his suggestion the company has used for twenty years, *"Non Refert Quam Multos Sed Quam Bonos Habeas."* In honor of the company's centenary this colophon is replaced this year by a new one which has been designed by Rudolph Ruzicka.

Herbert F. Jenkins, first vice president, entered the employ of the company in 1901 and has been associated with it ever since, first as advertising manager, later as head of the trade editorial department. Roger L. Scaife, second vice president, came

(*54*)

ALFRED R. MCINTYRE

from a long term of service with Houghton Mifflin Company, having first been affiliated with the *Atlantic Monthly*. John A. Reed, third vice president, in charge of trade sales and promotion, secured valuable experience in the retail field before joining the company. Henry G. Halladay, secretary, came to the company in 1898 when the Roberts Brothers business was acquired, and is in charge of manufacturing. Ross Whistler, treasurer, had valuable training for this office in the banking field and in various departments of the business. James W. Sherman, the youngest member of the Board of Directors, is in charge of the schoolbook department.

Some years ago a New York office was established, partly because the company has resident salesmen there and also because New York is the headquarters for authors and literary agents. Arthur H. Thornhill is in charge of sales; C. Raymond Everitt, who secured his publishing experience in the offices of Messrs. Harcourt, Brace and Company and later as New York manager of Curtis Brown, Ltd., literary agents, is the company's New York editorial representative.

In this century Little, Brown and Company has issued the books of many of the popular writers of the day, and has published many other books of which it is also proud even though their sales did not reach large figures. James W. McIntyre saw the possibilities of E. Phillips Oppenheim back in 1903, and a

E. PHILLIPS OPPENHEIM

happy and most successful association was begun which has lasted more than thirty years, and has led to a close friendship between Mr. Oppenheim and the younger McIntyre, who has regularly visited him, first at his villa on the Riviera, more recently at

Guernsey, in the course of his visits to Europe. Other favorite novelists who came to the company during the senior McIntyre's lifetime are Mary E. Waller, who wrote "The Wood-Carver of 'Lympus," Jeffery Farnol, author of "The Broad Highway," and A. S. M. Hutchinson, whose fourth novel, "If Winter Comes," published in 1921, achieved a sale of more than half a million copies in England and America within a year of publication. Mr. Jenkins discovered Thornton W. Burgess, whose animal stories for bedtime reading have been so popular with children. While Mr. Burgess was holding a modest editorial position in Springfield, Massachusetts, he began writing for his little son stories about Reddy Fox, Johnny Chuck and other familiar animals and birds. He was encouraged to submit them for publication, with the result that his first book, "Old Mother West Wind," was so successful that others followed until he had written over two score volumes. The popularity of the numerous Burgess books of animal stories has been truly amazing. The sales now total 4,350,000

(58)

A. S. M.
HUTCHINSON

THORNTON W.
BURGESS

copies. Through his books, his bedtime stories syndicated in scores of newspapers, and his radio nature broadcasts, Mr. Burgess has made his way into the hearts of millions of children.

More recently there have been the novels of A. Hamilton Gibbs and A. J. Cronin, important works in biography by Bernard Faÿ, Emil Ludwig and other writers, Charles Warren's monumental work, "The Supreme Court in United States History," which was awarded the Pulitzer Prize for history in 1923, and the most sensational success among War books, Remarque's "All Quiet on the Western Front." There is a story worth telling about this book. For a decade, following the War, publishers looked askance on manuscripts about the War, especially novels or narratives of personal experience. One day, early in 1929, Mr. Jenkins remarked to Mr. McIntyre that a revival of interest in the subject was about due. A few weeks later Mr. Jenkins produced a copy of the London *Observer* and showed Mr. McIntyre a despatch from Berlin which discussed the current popu-

CHARLES WARREN

ERICH MARIA REMARQUE

larity of German War novels and named half a dozen, among them *"Im Westen nichts neues,"* by Erich Maria Remarque. A ten-line description of this book was enough to convince them that they wanted it, and they cabled at once to a London literary agent. Another American publisher already had an option on the American rights, and had seen a portion of the translation; the story goes that he declined it (two days after Little, Brown and Company cabled) because it was pacifistic in tone. They cabled on March 1st; on March 4th they had secured the American rights. Other publishers wrote instead of cabling and were too late. "All Quiet" probably has been the most widely read book of our generation; in the space of three years, three and a half million copies were sold in the German original and the twenty-five or more translations.

On February 26, 1925, a forward step was taken that has proved itself to be even more important than the purchase of the Roberts Brothers business in 1898. It involved not only the addition of splendid books to the list but an association of a kind new in American book publishing. On that date Little, Brown and Company entered into an alliance with the Atlantic Monthly Company whereby Little, Brown and Company became the publishers of all Atlantic Monthly Press books, past, present and future as long as the alliance lasts. In 1908 the *Atlantic Monthly*, which had been owned by Houghton, Mifflin and Company, was sold by them to Ellery Sedgwick, who formed a new company, becoming its president and editor of the magazine. Some years later the company began the publication of books. In eight years it issued upwards of one hundred and twenty-five books, including "The Amenities of Book-Collecting" by A. Edward Newton; "Revolutionary New England: 1691–1776" by James Truslow Adams, which was awarded the Pulitzer Prize for the best work in American history in 1921; "Barrett Wendell and His Letters" by M. A. DeWolfe Howe, which was awarded the Pulitzer Prize for the best work in American biography in 1924; and the three sea

stories by Charles Boardman Hawes, "The
Mutineers," "The Great Quest" and "The
Dark Frigate," the last of which won the
John Newbery Medal "for the most distin-

A. EDWARD NEWTON

guished contribution to American literature
for children" published in 1923. All these
books hitherto issued by the Atlantic Monthly
Press were added to the list of Little, Brown
and Company, under a distinctive trade-
mark, as "Atlantic Monthly Press Books."

This happy association has been cemented by more than a decade of successful publishing. Among the "Atlantic" titles well known and enjoyed by the public may be mentioned the Jalna novels by Mazo de la Roche, the latest of the series to appear being "Whiteoak Harvest"; "The Hounds of Spring" and other English novels by Sylvia Thompson; "Rome Haul," "Drums Along the Mohawk" and other tales of New York State by Walter D. Edmonds; "Peking Picnic" and other novels by Ann Bridge; the Atlantic Prize Biographies, "Grandmother Brown's Hundred Years" by Harriet Connor Brown, and "Old Jules" by Mari Sandoz; Nora Waln's "The House of Exile," and James Truslow Adams's "The Adams Family" and "The Epic of America." Upon all these books, as well as many others, the Atlantic colophon is to be found. As a rule Atlantic books are initiated by the Atlantic editors, then a joint committee makes the publishing decisions and the Atlantic offices indicate the format in which the volumes are to appear. The processes of manufacture, advertising and distribution, however, are handled by Little, Brown and Company.

The sound judgment and the far-reaching contacts of the editorial staff of the *Atlantic Monthly* carry a prestige for the Press books which is unexcelled. This, with the long experience and high reputation of Little, Brown and Company in the production, promotion and sale of books of the best type, provides an ideal combination to furnish American book buyers with the best of literature. To this common enterprise there is a joint contribution of personal energies; Mr. Sedgwick and Edward Weeks, associate editor of the *Atlantic Monthly* and editor-in-chief of the Press, are primarily responsible for the Atlantic list, and the Little, Brown staff is as keenly interested in the success of this list as in that of its own. To the A. M. P. must go the credit for the great "Mutiny on the Bounty" trilogy of Charles Nordhoff and James Norman Hall, and for James Hilton's "Good-Bye, Mr. Chips," which most book publishers probably would have declined because of its shortness.

When Mr. Hilton visited Boston in 1935 he was entertained at a luncheon at which a group of headmasters representing the New

CHARLES NORDHOFF AND JAMES NORMAN HALL

England private schools were present and to them he recounted the beginning of this story.

It seems that by mere chance he met the editor of *The British Weekly* upon the street one day in the autumn of 1933 when he happened to be in London. They stopped to exchange greetings and the editor invited him to write a Christmas story upon the understanding that it be delivered in two weeks. To Mr. Hilton at that time the price offered — fifty pounds — was a considerable sum and he agreed, though with some hesitation because of the time stipulation.

Then he told of the mental torture, sitting at home vainly trying to capture a plot from his imagination and spending the first week without result. Panic seized him as time passed until one day he took his bicycle and wheeled out into the country, determined not to return until a plot had come to him. It was only at the end of the day as he was returning that the happy conception of Mr. Chips came to his mind. That evening he went to his typewriter, and in four days the story was written.

Ellery Sedgwick heard of the story, read it in *The British Weekly*, and bought it for the *Atlantic*. It was published in the April issue of 1934, and was so enthusiastically received that Mr. Sedgwick urged its publication as a small book. The book was published, and Mr. Hilton became famous. Those four days following the bicycle ride had changed the world for him.

In 1935 Little, Brown and Company took over the publication of *The Old Farmer's Almanac* and issued the 1936 Edition under their imprint. Published continuously since

1793, the Almanac is one of the most beloved of all American publications. It has annually reflected the sound core of rural life which exists beneath the overlaying of urban progress in much the same form as it did in the time of Robert B. Thomas, its founder. No change has been made in substance or appearance, the company believing that all the early traditions should be maintained. The distribution of the Almanac is handled entirely through the American News Company and its branches.

The publication of textbooks was a matter of small concern to Little, Brown and Company until 1904, when a separate schoolbook department was established.

A strong list of supplementary readers for the grades was soon secured and was everywhere accepted as outstanding. Later the house pioneered in the publication of textbooks in home economics, then called domestic science, a rapidly developing subject in the school world. In both fields the company had gratifying success.

"Speak! Read! Write!" by Elizabeth Crowe Hannum of Chicago. A second contest, for a high-school social science textbook, is now being held with the expectation that another preëminent book will result for that field of study.

The company's shipping warehouse and its bindery are in Cambridge. It was only natural that the firm should have turned toward Cambridge as a location for a bindery of its own. Its binding had been done by a Cambridge concern, Nourse and Company, which included in its partnership Messrs. Nourse, Frank Lemon and George Field, a brother of James T. Fields (who had changed his name some years previously). Furthermore, Mr. Little had extensive and varied interests in the city where his home was situated. Accordingly, in 1851, he negotiated the purchase of the land and buildings of the old Cambridge almshouse on Blackstone Street, and erected certain buildings, a number of which were subsequently sold to H. O. Houghton and Company and now form part of the Riverside

Press. On the north side of the street the Little, Brown Bindery was then erected, being designated "The Riverside Bindery." It is said that James Brown suggested the name of "Riverside" to Mr. Houghton, who likewise adopted it; thus the two institutions, the one Little, Brown and Company's Riverside Bindery, the other Houghton Mifflin Company's Riverside Press, have grown up side by side.

Prior to this date, the business of Nourse and Company had been taken over, and a new co-partnership formed with Mr. Lemon, which existed until Little, Brown and Company finally assumed full control. In 1902, the old buildings were replaced by the present structure, its facilities being supplemented by three warehouses for the storage of sheet stock. In 1920, this group of buildings was further augmented by the erection of a shipping warehouse, to accommodate the stock of bound books, which had previously been stored in the Boston office. In 1929, a substantial addition was made to the bindery building itself, almost doubling the plant's productive capacity. All these buildings are inter-connected, thus forming an admirable unit for binding, storing and shipping the bulk of the company's publications.

V

IN 1837 Andrew Jackson's successor took office a few months before Charles C. Little and James Brown joined forces. Jackson's second term had been a period of violent speculation. "Under the influence of a wild desire to grow rich without the toil of labor, men of every trade and occupation forsook their usual pursuits, hastened to the exchange and the auction block, and there risked the savings of a lifetime, the hoardings of a few years of prosperity, or the wealth from a former generation on the chances of a day or an hour. Shopkeepers, small tradesmen, clerks, factory hands from town and country, farmers, members of the learned professions, students in law offices, mingled with specu-

lators and capitalists to try their fortune."[1]
There was speculation in land, houses and
stocks; the state banks made borrowing easy,
there was inflation of the currency and prices
rose rapidly.

Martin Van Buren was inaugurated in
March, 1837, and "on the threshold of his
administration, he encountered a disastrous
business panic, the wild tumult of speculation
and inflation ending in an explosion. While
Jackson's war on high finance had doubtless
hastened the inexorable, it was not the sole
cause of the crash. The fact was that one of
the periodic cycles of capitalism was at hand
and the party in power could offer no effec-
tive remedies, if any there were. . . . The
government simply allowed the winds to
blow. Hundreds of banks failed; mills were
shut down; work on canals and railways was
stopped; thousands of laboring people were
turned into the streets; federal revenues fell
until a deficit supplanted a surplus; land
sales dropped off; and speculation came to a

[1] John Bach McMaster: "A History of the People of
the United States."

standstill."[1] Interest rates went to two and a half percent a month, failures in New York by the middle of April numbered one hundred and sixty-eight. "Book-printing stopped, furniture-makers discharged their hands, and people began to break up housekeeping. Trades unions, it was said, were nullified, and strikes no longer the order of the day. Provisions, wages, rents, prices, came down with a rush."[2] In May, the banks suspended specie payment, and Van Buren called an extra session of Congress for September first.

What were the hopes of Mr. Little and Mr. Brown when their new sign went up outside 112 Washington Street? Surely they were dubious as to the future. Little, Brown and Company has survived a century of booms and depressions, of growth and change. At the start of its existence the company went through one of the most severe depressions in the history of the country. In the concluding years of its first century the company has

[1]Charles A. and Mary R. Beard: "The Rise of American Civilization."

[2]John Bach McMaster: "A History of the People of the United States."

survived another period so similar that historians of the future may well deal with it in exactly the same phrases. To-day one wonders what is ahead as Mr. Little and Mr. Brown must have wondered a century ago. Perhaps they would not have believed that a business begun by them in a time of stress would still be using their names one hundred years later. They, and their successors, have regularly thought of the firm and later of the corporation as something more than a business organized and intended primarily for immediate profit. The present management, proud of the company's history, influenced in its daily actions by tradition, faces the future with confidence, convinced that democracy will survive in America and with it Little, Brown and Company.

A Few of the Famous Books
Published by
Little, Brown and Company

1839   COMMENTARIES ON EQUITY JURISPRUDENCE, by Joseph Story, one of nine great treatises by this eminent jurist. This was the Second Edition; the First was published by Hilliard, Gray & Company in 1836.

1842   A TREATISE ON THE LAW OF EVIDENCE, by Simon Greenleaf, the first great American authority on the subject. Publication was completed in 1853 when Volume III was issued.

1850–56   LIFE AND WORKS OF JOHN ADAMS, in 10 volumes, edited by his grandson, Charles Francis Adams.

1860   A TREATISE ON THE AMERICAN LAW OF REAL PROPERTY, by Emory Washburn.

1863   FAMILIAR QUOTATIONS, by John Bartlett. This was the Fourth Edition; the first three were published by Mr. Bartlett.

1865   PIONEERS OF FRANCE IN THE NEW WORLD, by Francis Parkman.

1868   A TREATISE ON CONSTITUTIONAL LIMITATIONS, by Thomas M. Cooley, a work which has never had a real competitor.

1872   A DICTIONARY OF ENGLISH SYNONYMES, by Richard Soule.

1881   THE COMMON LAW, by Oliver Wendell Holmes, Jr., still the greatest work on the common law by an American.

1881   COMMENTARIES ON THE LAW OF MUNICIPAL CORPORATIONS, by John F. Dillon. This was the Third Edition; the first two were issued by other publishers, the Sixth is now in preparation.

1890   THE INFLUENCE OF SEA POWER ON HISTORY, by Captain A. T. Mahan.

1896   QUO VADIS, by Henryk Sienkiewicz, the first of the best-sellers of the period.

1896   THE BOSTON COOKING-SCHOOL COOK BOOK, by Fannie Merritt Farmer, the leading American cook book.

1904   THE WOOD-CARVER of 'LYMPUS, by Mary E. Waller.

1904   A TREATISE ON THE ANGLO-AMERICAN SYSTEM OF EVIDENCE IN TRIALS AT COMMON LAW, by John H. Wigmore, the greatest American work ever placed before the American bar.

1910   OLD MOTHER WEST WIND, the first book of animal stories by Thornton W. Burgess.

1911   THE BROAD HIGHWAY, by Jeffery Farnol.

1915   THE INDIVIDUAL DELINQUENT, by William Healy, the pioneer book in its field.

1920   THE GREAT IMPERSONATION, the most popular of E. Phillips Oppenheim's 139 books.

1921   IF WINTER COMES, by A. S. M. Hutchinson.

1922   INTERNATIONAL LAW CHIEFLY AS INTERPRETED AND APPLIED BY THE UNITED STATES, by Charles Cheney Hyde.

1922   THE SUPREME COURT IN UNITED STATES HISTORY, by Charles Warren.

1925   THE ADVENTURES OF AN ILLUSTRATOR, by Joseph Pennell.

1927   JALNA, by Mazo de la Roche, the first of the Atlantic Monthly Press prize novels.

1929   ALL QUIET ON THE WESTERN FRONT, by Erich Maria Remarque, the most famous of all novels about the World War.

1931 THE EPIC OF AMERICA, by James Truslow Adams.

1931 HATTER'S CASTLE, A. J. Cronin's first novel.

1932 MUTINY ON THE BOUNTY, the first volume of the great trilogy by Charles Nordhoff and James Norman Hall.

1934 JOURNEY TO THE END OF THE NIGHT, by Louis-Ferdinand Céline.

1934 GOOD-BYE, MR. CHIPS, by James Hilton.

1936 DRUMS ALONG THE MOHAWK, by Walter D. Edmonds.

Some Famous Books
Published by Roberts Brothers
until 1898, then by
Little, Brown and Company

1868 LITTLE WOMEN, by Louisa M. Alcott, the favorite book of American girls.

1884 RAMONA, by Helen Hunt Jackson.

1884 DAILY STRENGTH FOR DAILY NEEDS, by Mary W. Tileston.

1890 POEMS (First Series), by Emily Dickinson. Second Series published in 1891, Third Series in 1896.

1891 POWER THROUGH REPOSE, by Annie Payson Call.